Green Smoothie Detox: The Best Green Smoothie Recipes for Good Health

Disclaimer and Terms of Use: Effort has been made to ensure that the information in this book is accurate and complete, however, the author and the publisher do not warrant the accuracy of the information, text and graphics contained within the book due to the rapidly changing nature of science, research, known and unknown facts and internet. The Author and the publisher do not hold any responsibility for errors, omissions or contrary interpretation of the subject matter herein. This book is presented solely for motivational and informational purposes only.

Table of Contents

Introduction 4

Introduction

A Smoothie is a thick smooth drink that is made of fresh fruit with milk, yoghurt or ice cream. Unlike the normal smoothies that people know, the green smoothie is dairy-free. Green smoothie is a thick drink that contains fresh fruits and dark green leafy vegetables like kales, spinach, parsley, broccoli, radish greens, beet greens etc. The smooth texture in the green smoothies comes from creamy fruits like bananas, papaya or mangos. The green smoothies are healthy as they are made from all natural ingredients. They contain vitamins, antioxidants and dietary fiber that come from the vegetables. If made well the green smoothie can contain 3-5 servings of fruits and vegetables which is the recommended daily allowance of fruits and vegetables.

Different Flavors Of Green Smoothies

There are different green smoothie fruit flavors that you can choose from. The fruit flavors include;

- Avocado
- Apple
- Apricot
- Black berry
- Blue berry
- Guava
- Grape
- Kiwi
- Lemon
- Lime
- Mango
- Orange
- Passion fruit
- Papaya
- And many more

To have these flavors in your green smoothie you will need to blend the chosen fruit with the other ingredients. Since the green smoothies don't contain any dairy content, they are good for the vegetarians. They are also good for all people regardless of the age.

Reasons For Taking Green Smoothies

Before you start taking the green smoothie you need to know the reason why you are taking the smoothie in the first place. Some of the reasons that might make you take the green smoothies are;

- The green smoothies are very nutritious; it is a known fact that green leafy vegetables are very nutritious. Once you take the green smoothie you will be taking a drink that is rich in vitamins and minerals. The leafy vegetables contain carotenoids that help in protecting your body from macular degeneration. They are also rich in folate that will help in protecting against heart diseases and cancer.

- Green smoothies are easy to digest; because they are in a liquid form, most of the fruits and vegetables are ruptured which make them to be absorbed easily.

- Green smoothies are easy to make; all you need is a blender and you will have the healthy drink ready.

- Green smoothies are an alternative to taking vegetables; most people especially children don't like eating vegetables. When you make the green smoothie you will not only take your vegetables but you will develop the habit of taking vegetables.

- Unlike other smoothies that have a high sugar content, green smoothie contains balanced sugar content. The vegetables you use dilute the sugar from the fruits.

Making a good smoothie depends greatly on the type of ingredients and the method used when making the smoothie. There are different steps that you can follow to help you make the perfect smoothie.

Step One: Choose Your Vegetables And Fruits To Use

There are a variety of green leafy vegetables that you can choose from. Ensure that you choose vegetables that are fit for you. When it comes to fruit, you can choose fruits that are sweet. It is a known fact that different fruits have different sugar content. Bananas are among the sweet fruit you can choose from. Just ensure that the banana is ripe before you use. There are other sweet fruits that you can choose from if you are not found of bananas. If it is your first time to make green smoothie, go for vegetables that are not too bitter e.g. spinach. You can choose to use spinach in combination with another vegetable like chard.

Step Two: Wash And Stem The Greens

Greens are very delicate, if stored with water they become soggy and rot quickly. So you should separate the green leaves from the stem by cutting off the stem and submerge the green leaves in clean water. Shake off the excess water from the leaves or leave them to dry before you store or use them.

Step Three: Add Liquid On Your Blender

This will enable the vegetables and the fruits to blend in quickly. You can choose any liquid including filtered water or coconut water. If you want to use the fruit juice, ensure that the juice is fresh and homemade. Don't use the juices from the store because they contain too much sugar and some have chemicals.

Step Four: Add You 'Base'

Your base is the fruit you will use to make the smoothie thick and smooth. The best base to choose is the creamy fruits like bananas or papaya. To add an extra creaminess to your smoothie you may add an avocado because the fruit is rich in good fat. Ensure that you chop the fruit before adding so as to make the blending easy. At this point you may add another flavor to the smoothie like strawberry.

Step Five: Add The Vegetables

After you have added the fruits and the flavor, add the chopped vegetables in to your blender. When you are adding the vegetables you can start with the soft vegetables like spinach followed by the tough ones like kales.

Step Six: Blend

Blend the ingredients together until the mixture is smooth with no lumps. It takes about a minute for the mixture to be smooth.

Factors To Note While Blending

- Depending on the type of blender you have you may be required to hit the pulses button for the vegetables to mix.

- It is only persons with Vitamix and blendtec blenders that are allowed to blend the fruits and vegetables together without chopping. The rest of the people you chop first.

- The blending time should last for only one minute. Don't overdo it or you will end up with a smoothie that does not have any nutrients.

Benefits Of Green Smoothie

There are many benefits that you will get to enjoy if you choose to start taking the green smoothie.

- It is believed that the green smoothie does help in weight loss. This is because the smoothies contain soluble fiber that is from the fruit and the vegetables. The fiber makes you feel full for longer hence you will not eat a lot of food. It also helps in weight gain through its high calorie content (this depends on how you made the smoothie).

- The green smoothie keeps you hydrated; it is recommended that you drink up to eight glasses a day. However, most people rarely take the recommended amount because of they don't like the taste. With the green smoothie, you will be taking in liquid that will keep you hydrated. Remember to however drink water because the green smoothie is not supposed to be taken as a substitute but as an addition to your normal diet.

- Green smoothie is very nutritious; when you take a glass you will get fiber which helps you lose weight and reduce cholesterol in the body. You will get antioxidants, phytonutrients, vitamins and minerals.

- It helps prevent kidney stones; in the recent past there have been many people claiming that oxalates in the green leafy vegetables may cause kidney stone. However a study that was done recently showed that the people who take low sodium foods have an increased probability of getting kidney stones. Kales are known to contain dietary calcium and low levels of oxalates. The dietary calcium is absorbed quickly in the body as compared to their counterparts, milk calcium.

- Green smoothie may rescue you from taking a fast food; when you feel hungry, it is advised that you take the green smoothie. The fiber in the smoothie will make you feel full hence restricting you from taking the fast foods.

- Green smoothie may help you ease the heat burn that is usually brought by indigestion. This is because the green smoothie are alkaline in nature thus they dilute the acid in the stomach.

- Green smoothie as mentioned above will help you take your vegetables without you noticing it.

- The green smoothie provides you with more energy and nutrients as compared to the separate fruit and vegetable juices.

- It is believed that when you take the green smoothie you will reduce you intake of the oils and salt.

- Green smoothie helps you to stop the sugar cravings. The smoothie contains about 3 servings of fruits which will help you stop your cravings as your body will not need the sugar.

- You are able to control your appetite; vitamins and minerals are known for controlling the appetite so when you take the smoothie, which is rich in the vitamins and the minerals, you will control your appetite.

- The green smoothie in addition to other factors may reduce the risk of heart disease. The smoothie contains high-fiber which is from the vegetables and fruits. Fiber helps to lower the cholesterol level in the body hence reducing the chances of having a heart condition.

- Your skins will be vibrant; dark green leafy vegetables contain cleansing and detoxifying agents which binds and eliminate toxins. They also help in developing healthy intestinal lining. So taking the smoothie will ensure your skin will be smooth.

- The green smoothie helps in reducing constipation through the fiber contained in the fruits and vegetables.

- The green smoothie can help you to detox your body; the green smoothies usually help you to detox through the chlorophyll contained in the greens you have used. The fiber contained in the fruits and vegetables also help to detoxify your body. The chlorophyll cleanses the body of all the toxins. It also helps to alkalize our systems by getting rid of the toxins. To start the detoxification process you are advised to take at least 2 glasses of the smoothie on a daily basis. When you start to detox you will experience some discomfort that is caused by the detoxification process however this depends on your body systems. Some of the detox symptoms that you will experience will be mild headaches, fatigue, low levels of diarrhea, bloating, and frequent bowl movements. As you continue with the process you will produce a smelly gas and also experience excess mucous. The symptoms are temporary and they will disappear after a while. Drinking a lot of water will help you in alleviating some of the symptoms.

- Green smoothies will help you to get better digestion; as mentioned, the green smoothie is rich in fiber which will help in moving food through the colon. The smoothie is contains enzymes which enable a smooth digestion and nutrient assimilation.

- You will get to experience mental clarity and focus once you start taking the green smoothie. The fruits and vegetables used are rich in vitamin B and potassium which are known for nourishing the nerves and the general functioning of the brain.

- The smoothies give you increased energy; they may not be high in calories, however the vitamins and minerals contained in the smoothie are easily digested hence they provide the cells in the body with energy.

1. Get More Out Of Your Smoothie

A green smoothie is still healthy with the fruit, vegetables and water. However, if you want to increase the calorie content of the smoothie you may add some boosters like protein powder. You may also include nuts (these are high in calories or chocolate in your smoothie. The chocolate will also provide you with antioxidants. Omega 3 seeds may also be quite beneficial.

2. Use Different Vegetables Every Time You Make A Smoothie

Different vegetables provide different nutrients and if you want to get the best of the green smoothie then you are advised to use different green vegetables in your smoothie.

3. Follow The 60/40 Formula

The formula represents 60% of the fruits and 40% of the vegetables. If it is your first time to take the smoothie then you should start with at least 70/30 as you build your tolerance to the smoothie. If you are making the smoothie for the children you should not include too many vegetables than the fruits as this will make the smoothie bitter.

4. Blend The Vegetables In Bits

You are supposed to blend the vegetables one after the other so that you can avoid any leafy chunks. The essence of blending the vegetable is so that you can save yourself the stress of chewing the vegetables. So ensure that they are mixed properly before drinking.

5. Don't Take Your Green Smoothie For Dinner

This is a bad idea because firstly, you will want to enjoy a normal meal with your family members. Secondly, if you take your smoothie for dinner you may experience gas and bloating especially if you took a regular lunch. This usually occurs because a regular meal take about 3-4 hours to be digested and absorbed in your body while the Green smoothies are absorbed instantly. This may cause bloating because your body will still be working on your lunch food by the time you take the smoothie. This will cause the smoothie to be held on your tract producing gas.

6. Use Natural Sweeteners To Make Your Smoothie Sweet

The recommended fruits to use are the bananas and the avocados because they are creamy and make your smoothie smooth. However, there are times when your smoothie is not sweet even after you use the bananas. You can add sweet fruits like oranges, strawberries, mangoes, or grapes to make the smoothie sweeter.

7. Start With Smooth Vegetables With Mild Sour Taste

When you are starting to take the green smoothie you should start with green vegetables like the spinach as they are mild in taste and tender. When you get used to the smoothie you may advance to the other types of green vegetables. The difference with spinach and vegetables like kales or parsley is that you cannot taste the spinach taste. With the kales no matter the fruit you use you will still taste the sour taste of the kales.

8. Make Your Smoothie In The Morning

It is advisable for you to make your smoothies when you wake up and then refrigerate. This will be convenient for you as you will not be going back to make the smoothie whenever you need it.

9. Take The Smoothie For Breakfast

There are some people who find it hard to take breakfast due to their busy schedule. If you are among those people you can take a smoothie especially the ones that have been boosted with protein powder. This will give satiety and make you feel full for until you get time to eat a regular meal.

10. Be Creative With The Green Smoothie And Keep It Simple

If your make a smoothie that is not tasty chances are you will not have the desire to make another one and you may discontinue taking the smoothie all together. It is thus important for you to learn how to make tasty smoothies so that you may be motivated to make the smoothie again. There are many smoothie recipes out there which you can choose from. Use your creativity and imagination to make the smoothie. The fact that you are using your imagination does not mean that you have to use all the ingredients you find in a recipe. You should use ingredients that you are familiar with. Use few ingredients when you are making the smoothie. This will help you not to use ingredients that you may be allergic to.

11.   Use Organic Green Vegetables Once In A While

Organic foods are rich in nutrients and they can be grown locally. Compared to the conventionally produce fruits and vegetables, the organic foods are more nutritious. The nonorganic vegetables may contain pesticides.

12.   Make The Green Smoothie Attractive In Appearance

The green smoothie is supposed to be green in color so add fruits like oranges or mangoes to brighten the green color. There are times when the smoothie might be brown in color especially when you use the watermelon and the strawberries. If you don't like the color you can change to a more attractive color like pink by adding beetroot to the smoothie or dark berries to turn it to purple. The taste will remain to be the same though.

13. Make Your Smoothie Sweet By Using Coconut Water

Instead of using the filtered water, you may choose to use the coconut water. This will add flavor to your smoothie. Coconut water is known to aid in weight loss because it acts as an appetite suppressant. It is also contains low levels of fat. Coconut water is also beneficial as it boosts hydration.

14. Use The Almond Milk

If you have the desire to add milk to your smoothie, you may use the almond milk instead of the regular milk. Almonds are rich in calcium. The almond milk will improve the general taste of the smoothie.

15. Take The Green Smoothie As A Meal Not With A Meal

Since the green smoothies are high in nutrients you can take them as a meal. Just ensure that you take a huge amount so as to provide satiety. Eating the green smoothie with food may cause some stomach upsets. This is because the regular food takes time to digest and absorbed and the green smoothie is absorbed instantly. The difference in the time between the two meals might cause bloating. It is also advised to take the smoothie on an empty stomach or after eating a fruit. You have to put in mind that the green smoothie is less in calorie and although it contains nutrients, you should take other foods in addition to the smoothie. However, you have to wait around 40 minutes after you take the smoothie to eat any food so that you can benefit from the smoothie.

16.   Don't Add Any Starchy Vegetables To The Smoothie

Starchy vegetables include carrots, green peas, pumpkin, beans, etc. The starchy vegetables don't mix well with the fruits. If mixed the smoothie may result in 'gas 4 less'. It is recommended that you use the normal ingredients of making a smoothie and only add the non-starchy vegetables.

Recipes That You May Use

There are many recipes out there on how to make the green smoothie. So you have a variety of options to choose from. Ensure that you choose a recipe that will work for you not against you. Below are four recipes that you may use.

1. The Green Smoothie Recipe

This recipe will give you your daily dosage of green vegetables. You can take this smoothie after you blend or you can take it as a frozen green smoothie pop.

Ingredients

- 2 ripe medium sized bananas

- 1 ripe pear or apple peeled and chopped (this is optional)

- 2 cups of chopped kales without the stems

- ½ of cold water

- ½ of orange juice (to sweeten the smoothie)

- 12 cubes of ice cubes if desired

Directions

- Take the bananas, pear or apple, kale and the orange juice and put them in the blender. Puree until the ingredients mix well.

- This recipe can produce about 2 servings each of 1 ¾ cup. If you want it to be a lot you can add water and bananas.

- Per serving the smoothie produce; 240 calories, 3g of fat, 55g of carbohydrates, 5g protein, 8g fiber, 38mg of sodium, 987 mg potassium, 0 cholesterol.

- The fruit exchanges was 2 ½ fruit and 1 exchange of vegetable.

2. Green Smoothie With Lime And Mango

Ingredients

- 2 cups of chopped and steamed spinach

- 1 ½ of frozen mango

- I cup of grapes

- 2 table spoons of fresh lime juice

Directions

- In the blender, put the chopped spinach, the frozen mango, grapes and the lime juice. Puree the ingredients until smooth. Add water while blending to reach the desired consistency.

- The smoothie can produce 2 servings.

- Per serving; 183 calories, 1g of fat, 32g of carbohydrates, 34g of sugar, 4g of protein, 5g of fiber, 33mg of sodium and 101mg of calcium, 1mg of iron.

3. **Green Smoothie With Avocado And Apple**

This smoothie is easy to make

Ingredients

- 1 ½ cups of apple juice

- 2 cups of chopped spinach or kale

- 1 apple chopped

- ½ avocado chopped

Direction

- Blend all the ingredients together until they are smooth adding water until you reach your desired consistency.

- The smoothie produces 2 servings.

- Per serving; 244 calories, 7g of fat, 3g of protein, 42g of carbohydrates, 28g of sugar, 33mg of sodium, 100mg of calcium, 2mg of iron.

4. Green Tea Smoothie

Ingredients

- 2 cups of baby spinach.

- 3 cups frozen white grapes.

- 1 medium avocado.

- 1 ½ of strong brewed green tea (use two tea bags to make the tea. The tea bag should not stay for more than 3 minutes).

- 2 tables spoon of honey.

Directions

- Combine all the ingredients together in a blender. Blend until smooth. You are supposed to serve this smoothie immediately.

- The smoothie makes about 2 serving of 3 ½ cups each.

- Per serving; 345 calories, 15g of fat, 56g of carbohydrates, 6g of sugar (added), 5g of protein, 9g of fiber, 36mg of sodium, and 1,110mg of potassium.

Printed in Great Britain
by Amazon.co.uk, Ltd.,
Marston Gate.